SOUTH WIND:
A Haiku Anthology

SOUTH WIND:
A Haiku Anthology

*Featuring the poetry
of HSA South Region members and friends
in celebration of the Haiku Society of America's
50th Anniversary*

Edited by David G. Lanoue
and Margaret Dornaus

Singing Moon Press
2018

Copyright © 2018 by Margaret Lane Dornaus

All rights reserved. This book or any portion thereof may not be reproduced or used in any manner whatsoever without the express written permission of the publisher except for the use of brief quotations in a book review or scholarly journal.

First Printing: 2018

ISBN: 978-0-9982112-1-3

Singing Moon Press
Ozark, AR 72949

Edited by David G. Lanoue and Margaret Dornaus

Front cover art by Jennifer Quillen *(rest in peace)*, from the haiga "the overlook trail . . ."

Distributed by: www.lulu.com

Contents

Editor's Foreword vii
South Wind Poems 10
Publication Credits 80
Index of Poets 85
Afterword 86

Editor's Foreword

Welcome to *South Wind*, a poetic celebration of the golden anniversary of the Haiku Society of America.

This book offers, all told, 105 haiku and seven *haibun* by 39 poets, seven of whom have passed away but whose lives and words we still cherish: Vaughn Banting, Carlos Colón, Ron Grognet, Leta Leshe, Bill Lerz, Jennifer Quillen, and Dr. Richard Paul Tucker. In addition, we offer several marvelous, original *haiga* selected by our publisher and book designer, Margaret Dornaus.

South Wind features poets from all five states of HSA's South Region—Arkansas, Kentucky, Louisiana, Mississippi, and Tennessee—and showcases haiku written by a few of our neighbors in Texas who technically belong to the Southwest Region, but whom we've happily adopted. In addition, the book presents contributions by members of the New Orleans Haiku Society's Yahoo Group, which includes friends from Idaho and North Dakota. Finally, we proudly feature two "Honorary Southerners," Fay Aoyagi of California (current president of HSA) and Shokan Tadashi Kondo of Tokyo. Fay and Shokan have earned this high distinction by kindly participating in, and contributing invaluably to, regional meetings of HSA-South held in New Orleans and in Hot Springs, Arkansas.

Speaking of Arkansas, I'm particularly delighted to offer poems by Howard Kilby, who for many years has organized and hosted haiku gatherings in Hot Springs, and by Johnye Strickland who, along with Howard, is one of HSA's living legends.

The past several years, I have spent a good chunk of my summers in Japan participating in *renku* led by Shokan.

This experience has inspired me to arrange the poems and stories in this volume according to the three-part structure of classical *renku*, haiku's literary parent. *Renku* starts much like a train slowly pulling out of a station: beginning with bright, innocent images, nothing shocking or disturbing. As the train of poetry gathers speed, it plunges forward into a middle section of verses that boldly explore what Shokan calls the "Mandala of All Creation": nature, the seasons, love, sex, war, sickness, drunkenness, politics, current events, animals, plants, monsters, birth, death . . . , and the glittering cosmos that cradles it all. Finally, in the third section, the train slows down, rolling to its destination of blossoms and enlightenment.

South Wind, you are about to discover, is strewn not only with striking gems of poetry in their own right but that in their sequencing and juxtapositions sparkle even more brightly, creating, I hope, something greater.

—David G. Lanoue
HSA Past President

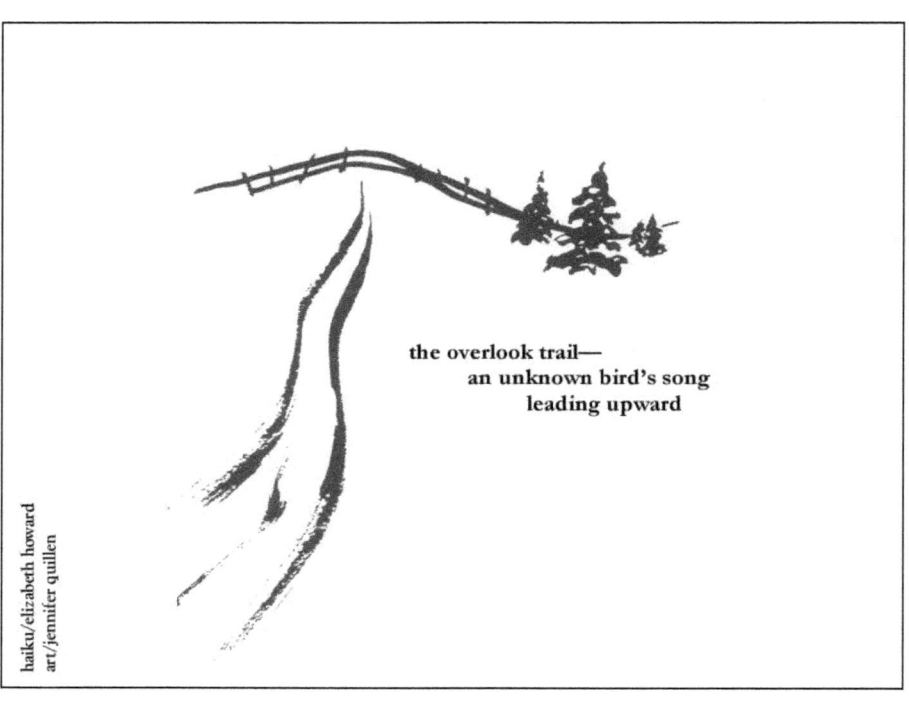

the overlook trail—
    an unknown bird's song
        leading upward

haiku/elizabeth howard
art/jennifer quillen

black south wind
a pirate ship
coming for me

    Fay Aoyagi
    San Francisco, California
    (Honorary Southerner)

winter dawn
    the sumi-e
of cloud shadows

        Johnye Strickland
        Maumelle, Arkansas

sitting meditation—
the cat's tail
feathers my back

        Samantha Klein
        Baton Rouge, Louisiana

in the garden
alone
song in the wind

    Carolyn Noah Graetz
    New Orleans, Louisiana

New Year's Day
the poisonous spider's
intricate web

    Juliet Seer Pazera
    New Orleans, Louisiana

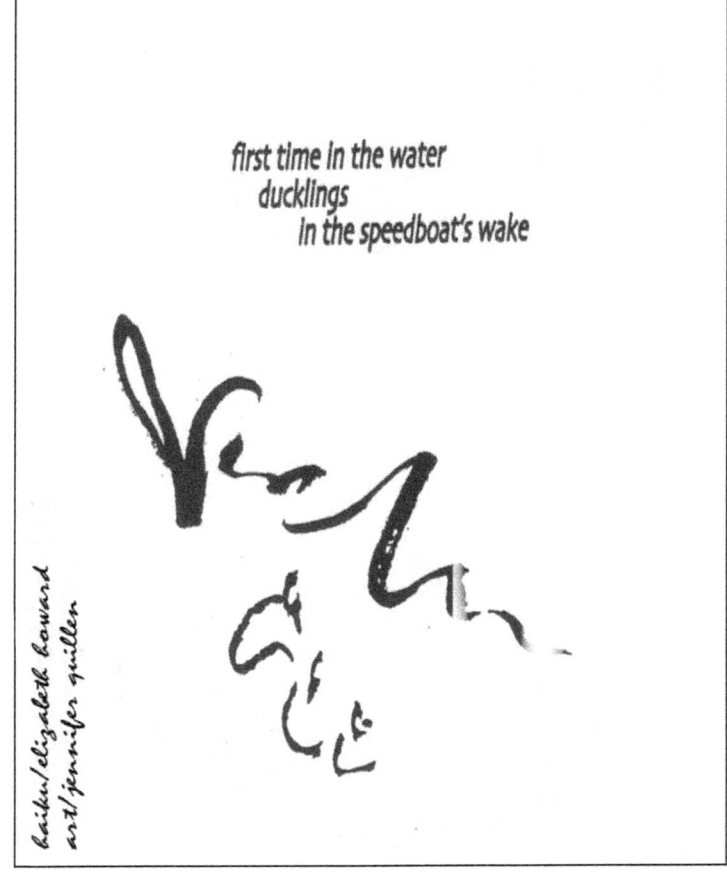

first time in the water
ducklings
in the speedboat's wake

haiku/elizabeth howard
art/jennifer quillen

mayapples
on the forest floor . . .
my secret self

    Margaret Dornaus
    Ozark, Arkansas

Baldwin piano
in the living room
the color of its sound

    Howard Lee Kilby
    Hot Springs, Arkansas

alone at the bus stop
she shifts her weight
no moon at all

    Theresa Mormino
    Hot Springs, Arkansas

runes and faces
carved into tree trunks
the baby sleeps

    Carole Johnston
    Lexington, Kentucky

meditation ends
in the prayer garden
a bumblebee

        Dennise Aiello
        Benton, Louisiana

all the poems
I've written
melting snow

        Carlos Colón *(rest in peace)*
        Shreveport, Louisiana

Big Bend Backpacking Trip

Vaughn Banting (rest in peace)
Metairie, Louisiana

I once took a five-day backpacking trip in Big Bend National Park with some friends. Our group first flew to Midland, Texas, where we rented a large station wagon to hold our backpacks, etc., and then drove it down into Big Bend country where we abandoned it in the middle of the desert and began our gradual ascent of the South Wall of the Chisos Mountains which rose straight up from the Rio Grande.

During the desert terrain portion of our trek, we followed an old Indian trail because the cactus was too thick to even consider bushwhacking. This fact also made it difficult to find places to lay our sleeping bags (tents were out of the question) and so we ultimately had to lay them end to end right on the trail itself to avoid puncturing them or ourselves.

It rained a little that night, and the next morning we woke to discover fresh cougar tracks on the path in among our sleeping bags. It seems that the cougar didn't like walking among the cactus any more than we did, and so he had delicately stepped between our bags on his nightly rounds.

> measuring
> with my palm
> cougar tracks at dawn

frozen together,
past and present—
winter wind

up the mountain
through black ashes
following pink lady's slippers

    Elizabeth Howard
    Arlington, Tennessee

    my reflection
        in the water
horsefly

    Carolyn Noah Graetz
    New Orleans, Louisiana

morning light
the beauty of spring
before my eyes

janet qually

long hot summer
the greenest
since my youth

        Johnye Strickland
        Maumelle, Arkansas

wild turkeys
warily down the hill
one then all

        Ron Grognet *(rest in peace)*
        New Orleans, Louisiana

dark avenue under the oaks
perfect
strangers

      David G. Lanoue
      New Orleans, Louisiana

one-year-old
with the iPhone
scrolling, scrolling

      Samantha Klein
      Baton Rouge, Louisiana

twentieth birthday—
the boogeyman
grows with you

    Nicholas M. Sola
    New Orleans, Louisiana

the slow rat tat
of fogdrops
in the magnolia

    Susan Delphine Delaney
    Plano, Texas

blood moon
I tell the voodoo priestess
to make a wish

    Juliet Seer Pazera
    New Orleans, Louisiana

Shadowy Park

Vaughn Banting *(rest in peace)*
Metairie, Louisiana

Before Hurricane Katrina one of the small pleasures in my life was to take my handicapped scooter and visit a small park not far from our home.

Apart from its other charms it provided a perfect place for me to indulge in my favorite hobby: writing haiku. Also, as a retired horticulturalist I had always been interested in dendrology, and this particular park contained quite an assortment of tree genera just begging to be investigated.

Each time before entering the park I was careful to stop off at a grocery store to purchase some peanuts for the squirrels. Feeding the squirrels, identifying interesting trees, and writing haiku under their graceful branches; that was me in the days leading up to Katrina.

I will always remember my first trip back into that park after all the broken and toppled trees had been cleared enough for me to gain legal access. So many trees had been blown down or ripped apart by the winds that it was now a totally different place. The sun shone down now unhindered by the once ubiquitous trees that had given the little park its magic.

> the only one left
> a squirrel jumps from
> branch to branch

we set up lawn chairs
to watch our neighbor's
house burn

    Nicholas M. Sola
    New Orleans, Louisiana

Simon says
take two steps back—
spring layoffs

    Karen O'Leary
    West Fargo, North Dakota
    (New Orleans Haiku Society
    E-Member)

from the witnesses
how the wreck did not occur
odor in the court

    Victor Fleming
    Little Rock, Arkansas

after the earthquake
no one found
behind broken prison walls

    Steve Sharp
    Maumelle, Arkansas

decorated cake
he licks the icing
off his Purple Heart

      Vaughn Banting *(rest in peace)*
      Metairie, Louisiana

empty bar stools
crowd
a silent drinker

      Steve Tabb
      Boise, Idaho
      (New Orleans Haiku Society
      E-Member)

Dead Sea salt bath
she refuses to discuss
politics

>   Juliet Seer Pazera
>   *New Orleans, Louisiana*

frozen moon
a dictator's uniform
out from the closet

>   Fay Aoyagi
>   *San Francisco, California*
>   *(Honorary Southerner)*

President Trump tweets
a nuclear reply
before breakfast

    Howard Lee Kilby
    Hot Springs, Arkansas

American eclipse
the sun's long black
shadow

    David G. Lanoue
    New Orleans, Louisiana

remnants of
his garden
heroin addict

    Juliet Seer Pazera
    New Orleans, Louisiana

at the hazardous
waste site
an eight-leaf clover

    Carlos Colón *(rest in peace)*
    Shreveport, Louisiana

strutting around
the old fort
a murder of crows

    Johnye Strickland
    Maumelle, Arkansas

how she decided
to become a sunflower . . .
Ground Zero

    Fay Aoyagi
    San Francisco, California
    (Honorary Southerner)

spacious window—
   sunflowers in the gold vase
      turning westward

haiku/elizabeth howard
art/jennifer quillen

late Christmas Eve
one lone pigeon
walking home

    Robert Allen
    Metairie, Louisiana

morning
after the bombing
the silent sand

    Sydney Bougy
    Memphis, Tennessee
    (Urbana, Illinois transplant)

solar eclipse
the blind dog
sniffs his way home

        Judy Michaels
        Maumelle, Arkansas

look at those birds
I'd like to be a sparrow
and just fly away

        Richard Paul Tucker *(rest in peace)*
        Hot Springs, Arkansas

Katrina Cleanup

Vaughn Banting *(rest in peace)*
Metairie, Louisiana

In Katrina's wake houses sat in polluted flood waters for weeks. When the water finally receded homeowners found themselves not only throwing out ruined furniture and large appliances but also personal belongings of nostalgic value. And as if all of this were not enough, they had to totally gut their homes. Gutting a home meant the removal of sheetrock from all interior walls and in a few situations even the siding from outside walls. In these extreme cases houses were simply reduced to their studs.

While all this was going on, FEMA representatives and insurance adjusters were combing the affected neighborhoods as homeowners stoically guided them through their ruined homes.

    seeing him
    through the house
    a refreshing view of the garden

flash flood
a toad on the doormat
drying out

      Elizabeth Howard
      Arlington, Tennessee

squirrel on a wire
his tail
in full ballet

      Samantha Klein
      Baton Rouge, Louisiana

today
my name is wind river
crow mind

> Carole Johnston
> *Lexington, Kentucky*

popping out
of the flood-watered laundry
a frog

> Samantha Klein
> *Baton Rouge, Louisiana*

just above
the sign EXIT HERE . . .
supermoon

    Margaret Dornaus
    Ozark, Arkansas

watching it
become something else
spring cloud

    Rebecca Drouilhet
    Picayune, Mississippi

hottest hour
last spoon of ice cream
liquid moment

    Marian M. Poe
    Plano, Texas

autumn sea . . .
the driftwood shapes
of old grief

    Rebecca Drouilhet
    Picayune, Mississippi

snow glare—
wild geese helter-skelter
seeking the route

> Elizabeth Howard
> *Arlington, Tennessee*

snowy trees
a white heron hones in
on the blue pond

> Elizabeth Howard
> *Arlington, Tennessee*

winter dusk
spiked black coffee
over ice

      Juliet Seer Pazera
      New Orleans, Louisiana

    into the   stone soup
        pothole

          Scott Billington
          New Orleans, Louisiana

blood and rust
color of a bird's heart
searching for song

      Carole Johnston
      Lexington, Kentucky

Delicate Marriages

Vaughn Banting *(rest in peace)*
Metairie, Louisiana

Marriage is a fickle thing. Often the contract begins as a document more concerned with its frilly borders than with its small print. But even founded on such unstable beginnings some marriages will grow and flourish, both parties bravely stepping over the crevasses that from time to time open up threatening to divide even the most God-blessed of unions.

Other marriages, however, with much firmer foundations will sometimes inexplicably slowly wither and die. But even in such failed marriages after time and growth there comes the opportunity to re-examine and look again with less judgmental eyes at that partner who at one time seemed to have had such an ugly nature.

>seeing her now
>in a different light
>no rush to get the candles

red roses
wilted
asleep in separate beds

    Nicholas M. Sola
    New Orleans, Louisiana

she bends low for a coin
streetcar
named desire

    David G. Lanoue
    New Orleans, Louisiana

wild mint
he gives in
a little

> Johnette Downing
> *New Orleans, Louisiana*

thin ice—
I meet
her parents

> Nicholas M. Sola
> *New Orleans, Louisiana*

tea leaves
I turn the cup this way
that way

      Johnette Downing
      New Orleans, Louisiana

warm eyes—
his tongue
goes on arguing

      Samantha Klein
      Baton Rouge, Louisiana

winter chill
a love song my father wrote
not to my mother

    Johnette Downing
    New Orleans, Louisiana

    island wedding
      fiery dancing
        into the night

        Steve Sharp
        Maumelle, Arkansas

spring fever
wrapped in his shirt
again

    Barbara Tate
    Winchester, Tennessee

honeymoon
the sweet taste
of coming rain

    Barbara Tate
    Winchester, Tennessee

riding the waves
of her hair
his fingers

    Karel Sloane-Boekbinder
    New Orleans, Louisiana

to a country not on the map
a butterfly
my companion

    Shokan Tadashi Kondo
    Tokyo, Japan
    (Honorary Southerner)

wedding reception
daddy's girl
dirty dancing!

      Mike Hebert
      Baton Rouge, Louisiana

after August rain
steamy tin roof
Tennessee's cat

      Emma Dutreix Pierson
      Kenner, Louisiana

small okra pods steamed bite off their heads

    Marian M. Poe
    Plano, Texas

rock garden—
the firefly's
last light

    Nicholas M. Sola
    New Orleans, Louisiana

Tea Sets

Vaughn Banting *(rest in peace)*
Metairie, Louisiana

In driving around the streets of New Orleans, the results of its recent flooding due to Hurricane Katrina leaves one with a pervasive sense of sadness. Those who had little before the storm now had even less; homes that once represented places of security now only reminded their owners of a deepening sadness.

In times such as these, some of us are led to believe that parts of society are somehow insulated from such catastrophes and that simply their station in life alone protects them from the mundane setbacks of the less prosperous. In Hurricane Katrina, I assure you this was not the case.

>among the tea sets
>and overstuffed chairs
>gutted homes of the wealthy

epiphany . . .
waking to
new fallen snow

      Margaret Dornaus
      Ozark, Arkansas

blossoming clouds
an old scarecrow
watches the sunrise

      Bill Lerz *(rest in peace)*
      Hot Springs, Arkansas

reading Issa
between the lines . . .
a winter fly

    Johnye Strickland
    Maumelle, Arkansas

another year gone
eyeing the changes
in the distorted mirror

    Theresa Mormino
    Hot Springs, Arkansas

family reunion
grandparents
boast once again

> Carolyn Noah Graetz
> *New Orleans, Louisiana*

Luray Caverns
seven million years old
my first senior discount

> Scott Billington
> *New Orleans, Louisiana*

bonsai garden
planted by old friends
so long ago

    Howard Lee Kilby
    Hot Springs, Arkansas

trees slowly
lose their voices—
falling leaves

    J. Andrew Lockhart
    Van Buren, Arkansas

old stuffed chair
we remind him
how his joke ends

      Johnette Downing
      New Orleans, Louisiana

white lace on the table Santa's eggnog

      Marian M. Poe
      Plano, Texas

morning fog
thick with distant
years

    J. Andrew Lockhart
    Van Buren, Arkansas

    juicy red
    tomato sandwich
    mayonnaise

        Marian M. Poe
        Plano, Texas

crack addict
another visit
to the chiropractor

    Scott Billington
    New Orleans, Louisiana

zen concert
an air guitar
slightly out of tune

    Carlos Colón *(rest in peace)*
    Shreveport, Louisiana

jazz combo's
second set . . .
the sound of crickets

    Steve Tabb
    Boise, Idaho
    (New Orleans Haiku Society E-Member)

driving late
on bluegrass backroads
the music of my home

    Carole Johnston
    Lexington, Kentucky

Wind Damage

Vaughn Banting *(rest in peace)*
Metairie, Louisiana

During Louisiana's two recent hurricanes many people sustained damage to their roofs. Fortunately most of this was limited to shingle loss, but in many cases trees fell on houses causing gaping holes in their roofs. This allowed rain to come in and soak furniture, paintings, carpets and walls, etc.

In response, FEMA representatives provided large blue tarps for the needy victims and eventually came around and securely fastened them to their roofs. This service provided at least an interim fix until roofs could be repaired properly by contractors. Nonetheless in most cases the damage had already been done. People lost their libraries, family albums, important documents, and treasured keepsakes. Due in part to these losses, the level of depression in most neighborhoods was palpable.

>in the mounting gloom
>every second house
>a blue roof

thinking I smell a cigarette
first anniversary
of mother's death

    Theresa Mormino
    Hot Springs, Arkansas

voter rolls—
your name no longer
next to mine

    Margaret Dornaus
    Ozark, Arkansas

pulling weeds—
my family reunion
at the graveyard

    J. Andrew Lockhart
    Van Buren, Arkansas

frosted pumpkin
the crows peck
a grin toothless

    Barbara Tate
    Winchester, Tennessee

his brilliant mind
held back by Alzheimer's—
the blue of his eyes

    Howard Lee Kilby
    Hot Springs, Arkansas

I move her jaw
to close her mouth
the coolness

    Johnette Downing
    New Orleans, Louisiana

Hiroshima Day—
a blister
from new sandals

>Fay Aoyagi
>*San Francisco, California*
>*(Honorary Southerner)*

>memorial
>so many empty chairs
>touched by moonlight

>>Margaret Dornaus
>>*Ozark, Arkansas*

speaking to us
the empty chair
at the poetry reading

      Carlos Colón *(rest in peace)*
      Shreveport, Louisiana

on the porch
a dead robin
the call I never made

      Theresa Mormino
      Hot Springs, Arkansas

Passover Moon . . .
the journey that begins
with this ending

    Rebecca Drouilhet
    Picayune, Mississippi

wrong number—
a stranger says
his final goodbye

    Elizabeth Howard
    Arlington, Tennessee

Trading on His Story

Vaughn Banting *(rest in peace)*
Metairie, Louisiana

After the flooding brought by Katrina and Rita, New Orleans found itself with a sudden shortage of automobiles; so many cars had been lost in fact that returning refugees came home to streets largely free of traffic. And unbeknownst to them at this point, when the storms had hit, nearly every car other than the ones they had escaped in had now been submerged in polluted flood waters for all the weeks they had been gone and were now completely beyond repair.

The twin storms had caused a mass exodus of people heading anywhere away from New Orleans, and like milkweed seeds cast to the wind, New Orleans residents found themselves far from their homes before traveling far enough to put some distance between themselves and the storms. Lodgings were difficult to find, and some had to stay with friends and family risking wearing out their welcome, while others simply relocated permanently. It seemed everyone who had evacuated had his or her own personal story to tell of their temporary self-imposed exiles.

Whether the people left in New Orleans were interested in them or not, and regardless of the fact that each New Orleans resident who had stayed in the city and not evacuated had his or her own very personal story to tell, every returning evacuee couldn't wait to share theirs and then rush off to barter for an automobile.

> at the dealership
> cashing in his story
> for a song and dance

the promise
still unfolding . . .
winter rainbow

    Rebecca Drouilhet
    Picayune, Mississippi

flowers begin
their morning stretch—
spring equinox

    J. Andrew Lockhart
    Van Buren, Arkansas

from the leaf
to my finger
a ladybug

    Steve Tabb
    Boise, Idaho
    (New Orleans Haiku Society E-Member)

silence
which follows the noise—
all saints day

    J. Andrew Lockhart
    Van Buren, Arkansas

frigid blue sky
Canadian geese
circling

    Leta Leshe *(rest in peace)*
    Shreveport, Louisiana

north wind
on the same branch
limes and icicles

    Dennise Aiello
    Benton, Louisiana

reflected
on the waxed linoleum
the waning moon

    Theresa Mormino
    Hot Springs, Arkansas

        sunset walk
        a pool of gold
        at the rainbow's end

            Barbara Tate
            Winchester, Tennessee

Backster effect
the African violet trembles
at my smile

    Johnye Strickland
    Maumelle, Arkansas

    pointing
    my way home
    the starfish

        Carlos Colón *(rest in peace)*
        Shreveport, Louisiana

Publication Credits

Haiku:

"at the hazardous . . ." Carlos Colón, *Point Judith Light* 2.2 (1993).

"autumn sea . . ." Rebecca Drouilhet, *The Heron's Nest* (June 2017).

"black south wind . . ." Fay Aoyagi, *Acorn* 31 (Fall 2013).

"blood and rust . . ." Carole Johnston, *Wild Voices* (2017).

"crack addict . . ." Scott Billington, *bottle rockets* 33 (2015).

"dark avenue under the oaks . . ." David G. Lanoue, *Paper Wasp* 14.4 (Spring 2008).

"driving late . . ." Carole Johnston, *hedgerow* 110 (2017).

"frigid blue sky . . ." Leta Leshe, *Ouachita Life Haiku Lines* (December 2014).

"frosted pumpkin . . ." Barbara Tate, *Frogpond* 37.3 (Autumn 2014).

"frozen moon . . ." Fay Aoyagi, *Mariposa* 36 (Spring-Summer 2017).

"Hiroshima Day . . ." Fay Aoyagi, *HSA Newsletter* (August 2017).

"honeymoon . . ." Barbara Tate, *Modern Haiku* 46.3 (2015).

"I move her jaw . . ." Johnette Downing, *Frogpond* 31.2 (Spring-Summer 2008).

"into the stone soup . . ." Scott Billington, *bottle rockets* 33 (2015).

"look at those birds . . ." Richard Paul Tucker, *Ouachita Life* (date unknown).

"Luray Caverns . . ." Scott Billington, *bottle rockets* 33 (2015).

"memorial . . ." Margaret Dornaus, *Prayer for the Dead* (Singing Moon Press 2016).

"old stuffed chair . . ." Johnette Downing, *bottle rockets* 33 (2015).

"Passover Moon . . ." Rebecca Drouilhet, *Modern Haiku* 46.3 (2015).

"pointing . . ." Carlos Colón. *RAW NerVZ HAIKU III* 1 (1996).

"the promise . . ." Rebecca Drouilhet, *A Hundred Gourds* (June 2015).

"red roses . . ." Nicholas M. Sola, *America's Greatest Otaku* (Episode 7).

"runes and faces . . ." Carole Johnston, *Akitsu Quarterly* (Winter 2015).

"Simon says . . ." Karen O'Leary, *Frogpond* 36.2 (Spring-Summer 2015).

"speaking to us . . ." Carlos Colón, *Sunday at Four* 8.3 (2001).

"spring fever . . ." Barbara Tate, *Modern Haiku* 48.2 (2017).

"strutting around . . ." Johnye Strickland, *Small Canyons* (2008).

"sunset walk . . ." Barbara Tate, *NeverEnding Story* (June 16, 2016).

"tea leaves . . ." Johnette Downing, *Modern Haiku* 41.3 (2010).

"thin ice . . ." Nicholas M. Sola, *cattails* (May 2014).

"to a country not on the map . . ." Shokan Tadashi Kondo, *Cherry Tree from Okinawa* (2017).

"today . . ." Carole Johnston, *Akitsu Quarterly* (Fall 2014).

"twentieth birthday . . ." Nicholas M. Sola, *cattails* (May 2014).

"watching it . . ." Rebecca Drouilhet, *Modern Haiku* 46.1 (2015).

"we set up lawn chairs . . ." Nicholas M. Sola, *cattails* (May 2014).

"wild mint . . ." Johnette Downing, *Modern Haiku* 41.2 (2010).

"winter chill . . ." Johnette Downing, *bottle rockets* 34 (2016).

"winter dawn . . ." Johnye Strickland, *Haiga Online* 11.1 (2010).

"zen concert . . ." Carlos Colón, *RAW NerVZ HAIKU III* 1 (1996).

Haiga:

"first time in the water . . ." Elizabeth Howard/Jennifer Quillen, *Voices and Echoes: HSA Members' Anthology* (2001).

"reading Psalms . . ." Janet Qually, *Minefields in Our Memory: A Spiritual Guide to Extracting Emotional Shrapnel (2017).*

"spacious window . . ." Elizabeth Howard/Jennifer Quillen, *Limestone Circle* 10 (Spring 2001).

"the overlook trail . . ." Elizabeth Howard/Jennifer Quillen, *summer dreams: American Haiku & Haiga* 3 (2002).

"tramp art . . ." Margaret Dornaus, *Haiga Online* 12.2 (December 2011).

Index of Poets

Dennise Aiello 17, 74

Robert Allen 35

Fay Aoyagi 11, 30, 33, 68

Vaughn Banting 18, 26, 29, 37, 46, 55, 64, 71

Scott Billington 44, 58, 62

Sydney Bougy 35

Carlos Colón 17, 32, 62, 69, 77

Susan Delphine Delaney 24

Margaret Dornaus 15, 41, 56, 65, 68, 75, 78

Johnette Downing 48, 49, 50, 60, 67

Rebecca Drouilhet 41, 42, 70, 72

Victor Fleming 28

Carolyn Noah Graetz 13, 20, 58

Ron Grognet 22

Mike Hebert 53

Elizabeth Howard 10, 14, 20, 34, 39, 43, 70

Carole Johnston 16, 40, 45, 63

Howard Lee Kilby 15, 31, 59, 67

Samantha Klein 12, 23, 39, 40, 49

Shokan Tadashi Kondo 52

David G. Lanoue 23, 31, 47

Bill Lerz 56

Leta Leshe 74

J. Andrew Lockhart 19, 25, 59, 61, 66, 72, 73

Judy Michaels 36

Theresa Mormino 16, 57, 65, 69, 76

Karen O'Leary 27

Juliet Seer Pazera 13, 25, 30, 32, 44

Emma Dutreix Pierson 53

Marian M. Poe 42, 54, 60, 61

Johnye Strickland 12, 22, 33, 57, 77

Janet Qually 21, 38, 45

Jennifer Quillen 10, 14, 34

Steve Sharp 28, 50

Karel Sloane-Boekbinder 52

Nicholas M. Sola 24, 27, 47, 48, 54

Steve Tabb 29, 63, 73

Barbara Tate 51, 66, 76,

Richard Paul Tucker 36

Afterword

Fifty years ago Harold G. Henderson and Leroy Kanterman founded the Haiku Society of America to promote the writing, reading and appreciation of English language haiku. Twenty-three charter members attended the group's first meeting, held in New York City in 1968. And 10 years later, the society began publishing its signature journal *Frogpond* as a way to showcase the work of a growing community of haiku poets, scholars and enthusiasts.

Thanks to the society's legacy and early leadership, English language haiku has grown by leaps and bounds during the ensuing 50 years. HSA's mission has encouraged poets to keep pushing the boundaries of the haiku form by offering members a shared community where they can walk their personal haiku path as they explore a wide-ranging, communal haiku world.

It's in that spirit—of gratitude and appreciation—that the members of the HSA's five-state South Region offer this diverse collection of haiku, haibun and haiga, made possible, in part, by a special anniversary grant from the Haiku Society of America. We hope you enjoy *South Wind*'s contribution to HSA's half-century celebration!

—Margaret Dornaus
HSA South Region Coordinator

www.ingramcontent.com/pod-product-compliance
Lightning Source LLC
Chambersburg PA
CBHW032208040426
42449CB00005B/486